Spiritual Verse Today is an inspirational read from Award-Winning #1 Best-Selling author **Sharon CassanoLochman**. Thousands have found daily comfort and hope through her poetic verse and the powerful words offering a gentle nudge towards peaceful tomorrows.

Spiritual Verse Today addresses inspirational heartfelt reflections—snippets of time. Lifting troubled souls from the heaviness of life that sometimes drags from behind. Distractions that tug at the heart left untended. Sorrows overwhelming even on the brightest of days. Find hope for the future, forgiveness for the past, and peace in the moment.

Join author Sharon CassanoLochman for a walk in *God's Light, Spiritual Verse Today*.

Spiritual Verse Today

Gifted Time

VOLUME III

SHARON CASSANOLOCHMAN

Ontario Shore Publishing
PO Box 453
Kendall, NY 14476

Cover design by Debbie O'Byrne.

To Fumihiko Nishimura
—Thank you for finding your way to my home and my heart. You are the gentlest of souls and a keeper of a mother's love.

Dedicated to the memory of my mother and grandmother. May your spirit live on through my words and actions as I remain keenly aware of gifted time.

Table of Contents

Author's Note

Extend beyond the comforts of your space and self today. Buy a cup of warm coffee and a sandwich for a homeless person. Donate extra clothing. Hold the door and gift a good morning exchange. Stop and recognize the daily interactions that slip away moment by moment. Life untended goes by without notice.

Waste not one moment chasing after the next.

Gifted Time. There are no guarantees for our length of stay. Be the best. Love the most. Smile the widest. Share in this moment of gifted time God's graces.

—Sharon CassanoLochman

GIFTED TIME

Weighty Steps

How weighty is the human step. Forging highways or great divides.

How resilient is the human heart. Forging bonds or shutting others out.

Humbly walk. Humbly love. Humbly think. For weighty are the steps of man passing through on gifted time.

Friends of Substance

Confused you have been. Giving of yourself and heart. Believing in the bond called friendship. Sharing intimate details of life's dramas. Then like the wind, your friend changed course. How could this be? You were so close. . . .

The world is full of papier-mâché friendships. Fragile and without substance. Tumbling and blowing in popular direction. Some called acquaintances. Others drawn to your heart. So difficult to understand when disappointment grabs hold. When the hollowness is exposed.

Take heart, my friend. Bring God to your side to share the moments of life. Then others will follow. Solid in beliefs. Bright in Light. Parallel paths you'll take. Friendships of substance will follow.

Be grateful for hollowness exposed. Find God. Find your Light. Friends of substance will follow.

GOD IN THE MIDDLE

Union of Hearts

I've shared the roller-coaster ride. Caught along the earthly terrain of desires. The more that comes in, less of a union left behind. Pulled in opposing directions as two once acting as one, now throw emotional currency into an open-bottomed pot.

My friend, money is not the answer. What you have cannot be bought.

Take not for granted the union of hearts. Universally strong when united in Light. Self-assured, industrious, and kind.

Combined energies of two make a heavenly union of one. Get off the ride. Experience life. Run. Play. Read a book. Do the crossword puzzle together at night. Make time for each other. Bring God into your life. Take away the drudgery of earning a living *by living*.

Love life and each other with God in the middle.

SPIRITUAL GROWTH

Lessons Learned

Similar we are yet so different. Individuals maneuvering challenges. Intermittently intersecting paths. Tending life's verses. Spiritual growth at hand.

Perception is the key to growth. Growth through example. Growth through grit. Growth as a spiritual being is tough. No life manual. Reflection. Discernment. Integration.

Matters not the lessons presented. Matters solely progression. Give gratitude for life lessons learned. Inhale deeply after each interlude.

Patience required for yourself and others. Similar we are, yet so different. Anger, fear, and intolerance are dismantled with intentions compassionately driven.

SHROUD OF HUMANITY

Courage to Live

Surely there's more to life than watching the escapades of others. Wasted moments, wringing your hands. Hostage to your home. Hostage to life.

You live your life like that of a mouse. Timid and afraid. Scampering from window to window peeking through life's blinds that cover your pain. Easier to look out than to look within.

It takes courage to live an earthly life. Courage, my friend.

Set your intention with motion. Monumental leaps will abound if you take the first step. Step out of yourself. Cast aside that which once was—a mannequin covered in the shroud of humanity.

One small step. Lift your heart to the Heavens. Do not focus on the could-have-been. Focus on the now. Make a difference in this world. Make a difference for you.

Look inward. Look upward. Look to fill your heavy heart with love, compassion, joy, and happiness. Look to God. Mind not the actions of others. Take action with yourself.

Smile. Be happy. Step out of yourself and into God's Light.

HUMBLE HEART

Balanced in Grace

So much time you spend seeking acknowledgment through accumulations. Wealth, cars, homes, and vacations. Those things are wonderful. Comforts aiding the passage of time. But greatness is not determined by your station in life. Greatness is determined by the print you leave behind.

Greatness comes from a humble heart. Greatness comes from giving and receiving. Balanced in efforts. Balanced in grace. Search for *your* God. Worship on your knees. Look beyond the stoop of your doorstep. Look beyond the car you drive. Spread your arms to the sky.

Greatness is charitable acts gifted without the spotlight. The world does not revolve around accumulations, but as a whole of humanity in spinning continuation. Give of yourself, whether you help one person or reach a million.

Join me in prayerful exchange. Join me in creating a footprint of the most humble kind. Greatness is determined by *your* spiritual life.

POWER OF PRAYER

As One

The sense of urgency weighed heavily with our last encounter. Standard conversations withheld. Sharing convictions. Together. Holding tight to the helm. Approaching head-on an impending storm. Rocking the ship. Reaching for souls left alone and adrift. Behold the Light beyond the charcoal-darkened sky.

Today. Together. Join hands and hearts as well. Matters not your faith, age, or nation. Pray for yourself. Pray for each other. Join hands. Join hearts. Together we will weather the storm, leaving not one soul drifting alone. Reach for a neighbor, friend, or stranger. There's power in prayer. Join together in God as one.

LOOK TO HEAVEN

Praise

My heart weeps for your satirical edge. Gifted ribbon-wrapped curt remarks sent sailing around. Causing great sorrow and emotional scars. To what purpose does it serve? To what end do you expect?

What births such flagrant disregard?

A wonderful life of abundance awaits.

Let go of the edge that cuts another. Be witness to God, good deeds, kind acts, and heavenly praise.

Let compassion reflect from words spoken. Ask and accept daily support from Heaven.

LIFE STINGS

Console with Prayer

I'm sorry you grieve for life's challenges that come to pass. Sometimes life stings like the gusts of winter wind driven across an unprotected face. Be grateful for the sharp and abrasive moments of life. Open your heart and look for the beauty and perfection cradled in those moments of time.

Look to the Heavens and acknowledge the rainbow of hues painted across an endless sky. Search the darkening clouds for breaking rays of hope, beauty, goodness, and peace.

You are not alone. Console yourself with prayer.

RELEASE YOUR BURDENS

The Awakening

Take your burdens to the highest mountain where the air is freshest and the sun brightest. Allow the biting breeze to pinch your cheeks and fill your lungs. Set your soul free to soar through the clouds. Release yourself from the gravity of humanity and earthly ties that bungee you to the tarmac, constraining you amidst the pain and cruelty of humankind.

Nestled above human limitations, witness the life and breath of Earth Mother. See how she empties her lungs into the mountain breeze. Feel her force as she tends to each rock or grain of sand.

Go to the mountaintop. Tread lightly. Walk softly as not to disturb her mantra. Speak lovingly, for she hears your voice and tone. Offer respect and gratitude, for her bounties are as vast as her oceans. Hear the pound of her heart as waves rush a stony beach. Feel the purity of her existence. Give gratitude, for her life offers life to you in return.

Recognize that every speck of dust carries weight and substance as every dot upon a page holds something of value. Every word and thought are here for a reason.

Come down from your mountaintop. One foot deliberately placed in front of the other. Tend to your task, the mission you were entrusted to complete. Do it without ego. Do it not for fame or fortune. Do it for the collective good of all. The Universe awaits your awakening.

Believe in yourself. Believe that one small voice can move a nation. One small voice with heavenly inspiration can change the direction of humanity for the collaborative good of all.

You have a voice. You have a mission. You have a path. One step at a time. Gently tread.

Every dot and dash upon this page holds value. Every word and thought are here for a reason.

Dash . . . dot . . . dot. . . .

SHIFT OF FORCES

Positive Change

There is a shift quickly approaching. Hearts linking. Hands holding. Prayers mutating. Compassion offered regardless of differences of color, nation, or religion. Encompassing unity of the whole. Not the singularity of the individual. The whole. Together . . . united.

Join. Demonstrate change of a positive nature. Look not to the face of another but their heart. Seek what God sees beneath the human cloak. Reach. Hold. Overwhelming joy and compassion when the connection is made. Linked in heart, hand, and prayer. Link with another. Pray for the whole of humanity.

Demonstrate change of a positive nature. It is contagious.

DAWN OF A NEW DAY

Beauty in All

Today is the dawn of a new day. Let go of your burdens—do not live in the past. Forgive yourself for things left undone. Learn from yesterday. Rejoice in the wonders that envelope the moment. Challenge yourself to look for good and beauty in all and yourself.

HARDNESS OF HEART

Liabilities to God

S adness I carry over your hardness of heart. Kindness to others cast upon a shelf. Dusty and dirty from lack of use. Holding compassionate actions at arm's length. I see who you are. Do you? Tender and graceful shines your Light . . . yet your earthly shell dispels another.

Emotional torture of others is not the assignment here. Compassionately driven is a more honorable mission. If life's journey ends tomorrow, what burdens take you to the grave? What sorrowful existence has precious life yielded?

Change the exterior. Breathe in fresh possibilities. Give the shameful liabilities to God. Live the rest of your days in grace.

GIFTS GRANTED

Blessings Await

You spend your life seeking. Fabricating shallow happiness for that which you cannot see. Looking for someone or something to fulfill a need. Wasting precious time and energy. You spend your life striving for this or that and fail to recognize gifts previously received.

It is not hard to change your vision. From seeker—to seer—to believer. Look for the bounty ready to reap. Look beyond the superficial. See the wheat-colored fields bending and swaying to the rhythmic beat of the seasons. The gift of a winter day. The gift to do better. To be compassionately driven. To openly cry at the beauty of a butterfly. The gift to witness God's Light.

Each breath and step taken is a gift.

Spend your life seeing instead of seeking. Blessings and gifts await at your feet.

Peace amongst Chaos

Prayers for you I shall initiate. Never ending it is. Greedy for peace amongst the chaos. Grasping for hope. Burdens of the children weigh heavily upon the parental heart. Matters not the age or reason. Fear harbored for the collision with their crooked-trail decisions.

Change direction for them you cannot. Stop blaming yourself and others. Their path is as *they* must determine. Release to God your precious cargo once carried. Trust in God. Lessons of life will have meaning like a great manuscript unfolding. Each lesson personally experienced. For through the swallows and hills are gifts hidden—even along crooked trails. Joy, laughter, *and* sorrow happen for a reason.

Pray for peace amongst the chaos. Offer gratitude for hidden blessings unfolded. Open your heart to healing and trust. Embrace hope. Pray for clarity. Pray for the children. Pray for yourself. Pray for the unknowns. For each must take their own bumps and falls.

Boundless Beauty

Teacher you are of many sorts. That of the mind and the heart. All that you do shines as boundless beauty. God graces your life and all that you touch.

You are peaceful compassion and soulful exchanges. Child-like play and chatter. Billowing laughter with warm embraces. Intellectual conversations laced with good wishes for the human race. Always in your company I am safely wrapped.

With you the world is a much better place. Thank you for exuding beauty, integrity, and grace. The power of your goodness is truly contagious. I am blessed to call you friend.

TOLERANCE REQUIRED

Sacred Moments

Gentle reminder. To your heart-place go. Children of God come from all nations. Different in name, language, location, and religion. Tolerance required.

Honor beliefs carried within and those of others. From God a breath we have been gifted. Recognize our connectedness through worship. Care not what time of day or the manner in which another prays. Care *that* they pray.

In your sacred moments, send goodwill and wishes to those beyond your walls. To neighbors, friends, and unknowns. Lift this world through humbleness. Through love, compassion, and tolerance.

SIDELINES OF LIFE

Calm Waters

Helplessly I sit. A spectator from the sideline of your life. Consoling with words. Private moments in prayer. Acutely aware of actions and intersections that fuel the momentum. Prayers and blessings offered are not enough. The change must come from you.

You are the captain of the journey traveled. If circumstances have manifested a storm—change course. Let go of that which anchors you to the situation. Navigate your Earth walk to a different location. Allow God in your heart. Follow His Light to the calm waters of life.

LINKING OF HEARTS

Prayerful Reflection

It's all coming together. This path. The talk. The walk. Lessons slowly seeping like a drain gently unplugged. Patience required. It will all have meaning. Look for the unity of like-mindedness. Linking of hearts through prayer.

This planet has potential. Its people. Its destiny. Hold tight to ideals. The goodness of souls. Power of prayer.

When the closure of your day nears, drop to your knees. Offer gratitude. Visualize your blessings. Visualize this planet. Earth Mother healthy. Unity of hearts through laughter, good deeds, and prayerful interactions.

Belief in as much as a mustard seed. Belief. Prayer. Hope. Trust. God.

Messages of Hope

You are a borrower of words. Words gifted to you from God. Gifted to share. They are not yours to judge or covet. Do not cling to them as earthly trinkets. You are solely the messenger. This is your Light.

Do not waste time tending what does not belong to you. Write them and release them. There is a purpose to all that you do. Patience. Time. Motivation. Your efforts will cultivate the seeds planted.

Send forth heartfelt messages of hope. Cast them to the wind to be carried on the wings of angels. Allow your words to scatter untethered by time, space or place.

They belong to the souls that await the message. Your words have a destiny.

This is your Light.

HUMBLY ACKNOWLEDGED

Purity of Soul

I understand the place from which you come. You walk through life in darkness, fenced among humanity yet alone with the vision of a blind man. Your life abundantly full. Surrounded by friends and family. Busy you are, morning to night. Busy with good tidings and earthly accomplishments. But you find yourself yearning for more. Yearning for clarity and understanding of that which is grander. Grander than the last promotion. Grander than a baby's first breath.

Crazy, you think to yourself. What else can there be? What else, separate from that which you know? Separate from this which you live. Day-to-day. This. Simple. Basic. Existence.

But, dear one, there *is* more. There is more to life. More to you. More than accomplishments. More than promotions, bigger houses, and better cars.

There's you.

You are the grandest of that which is. You.

You are the perfection of God's love. Peace, serenity, and joy. Search no more, for you simply need to open your eyes. Look within yourself. Humbly acknowledge the beauty and purity of your soul. God created you. God gave you breath.

Find peace, dear friend. Find peace within your soul.

Gossiping Ways

Did you not find me silently sorrowful? Sobbing in my life's realities?

How so then is it that you sit in judgment of my personal decisions? Choices that are based on my life and not yours?

Humorous and hurtful rantings grouped together. Voices gathering momentum through malicious campaigns. Used you were, with listening ears. Unable to reflect upon your own debris-scattered life.

So you took to mine.

Mind your fences and I shall mind mine.

Facing Fears

What fears do I hold
just below the laughter
anchored to a soul that fights for life?
I fear. . . .
To be a dreamer without dreams.
A writer without a pen.
A mother without her children.
A singer without a voice.
An instrument that cannot play.
Alone in my circle, without.

I fear
I will fall back to sleep
Before realizing my purpose.
But I AM. . . .
I AM awake.
I AM never alone.
I will never be without.
As long as I have breath
I hold life, hope, voice, purpose, and God's Light.

WRAPPED AND SEALED

Golden Memories

Angst I feel for the space between. Distance comes in many forms. That of the heart. Sometimes location. Longing for idle chatter. How are you? What's new? Phone calls home. Miss you I do.

Dauntingly, time quickly passes. The cycle approaches nearing the end of *my* time. Unchanged you remain in attitude.

Gifted to you, my friend. Golden memories wrapped and sealed. Delivered through nature on the wings of a butterfly. Across waves of emotion.

Forever may you peruse the shades and hues of fields and skies. Reminders of smiles shared. Love everlasting. Pleasantness.

Life is short. Miss you I do.

CROSSROAD OF LIFE

Spiritual Ladder

You stand at the crossroad of life, looking left and then to the right. Asking for direction from any passerby willing to listen. Who knows the road best to take? Who has an interest at stake? Who benefits from giant strides of faith? My friend, the only person suited to offer direction—is you.

Sit quietly with yourself. Look for the street signs God has provided. Listen with your heart. The answers are there if you will only trust in your abilities and talents. You are here for a reason. What is your mission? Only you can provide the answer.

When insecurities arise, remember your lineage. Child of God full of grace, listen to the voice that comes from within. You are meant to shine. Shine *your* light on the path you are destined to take. You don't need to see where the road ends. You just need to see far enough to put one foot in front of the other. Leave hesitation behind. Forward and upward movement is required to travel the spiritual ladder.

FOGGY WATERS OF LIFE

Lighthouse Beacon

You've spent your life navigating the pounding and storming waters of life. Uncertainty, self-doubt, and self-inflicted abrasions have left you adrift in the foggy waters of life. You've run your course. Feeling lost and defeated.

My friend, you can re-route. Change your direction!

Look to the lighthouse beacon. Steadfast and grounded. Guiding through the foggy-laden waters of your life.

Look, dear one, for the Keepers of God's Light. Strategically placed. Lighting a path until you're able to shine your own beacon.

Mend your ship. Heal your heart. Change direction! Look for the beacon of God's Light of which you have always been gifted.

ABANDONED AT LIFE'S GATE

Innocence

So consumed are you with that which devours time with scurry. Head spinning whilst life spins out of control.

Your inner child, full of innocence and joy, sits abandoned at life's gate.

Stop, my friend. Stop for a mere moment. Go to a safe place sequestered from watchful eyes. Lift up your arms to the Heavens and give thanks for your life. Then dance. Dance in the darkness until you're able to dance in the Light.

Your child from within is knocking at the gate. Let in the child. Let in the Light.

You are a child of God's. You are *still* full of life, love, and innocence . . . if you will just open the gate.

Release from Sadness

I helplessly watch as you carry yourself on a sea of sadness, floating away from life's most precious moments.

Untidy your heart. Scatter and dismiss those things you hold closest that feed your sadness. Toss life's negativities to the breeze. Release self-indulging and self-destroying memories that keep you from your life destiny. Memories you covet through fear. Fear of hurt, judgment, shame, or loss. Memories deposited from your head to your heart. Buried and neatly organized. Buried in your most sacred place. Your heart.

Tidy and neatly organized compartments, ready to arm yourself within a moment's notice for mental or emotional battle. *I remember when* . . . as you pull from one compartment or another. *I'll never let that happen again.* You hide behind your earthly façade of false notions and false emotions. False emphasis on what is truly important.

But wait, what are you missing through your clouded, tearful vision? Could this be a good experience, a life lesson, a moment of brightness now denied to your soul?

Imagine yourself with closed eyes and hands tied behind your back. Imagine finding your way through life with the guidance of your heart and the knowledge that comes forth from within. Imagine floating on a rainbow-colored sea of hope, peace, and serenity. Enjoying the moment. Enjoying life without fear. Enjoying the solely-wondrous anticipation for what is yet to come.

Imagine finding the serenity of the moment through your heart.

Self-Reflection

So eager was I to end your discomfort. Anxiety painted across a China-glass face. Robbing you the gifted life lesson. Swiping it away with a misdirected good intention.

Arrogant, shallow, and inconsiderate was I. My intervention delayed the education you were intended.

Now with reflection, I humbly see my direction.

How clever of Him to help me *see* who the lesson was intended.

IGNORING TOMORROWS

Live for Today

Common it is. Putting off until tomorrow. Delaying that which could have been done today. The phone call to your beloved grandmother confined to bed. Donation to a shelter. Finishing the manuscript so nearly done. Might a better way be doing instead of procrastination?

Create the moment now instead of waiting for tomorrow. In a world of tomorrows how much has gone by? Waiting *to do* leaves a space void of you. The you that is needed in this place of intersecting goals and actions.

Leave not one moment void your gifts and talents. The tone of your voice long distance. Food and money donated with prayerful good wishes. The book propped on knees of children.

Allow space for action in each moment. Leave not this life a diary of procrastination. Leave substance. Love. Generosity. Imagination. Creation. Create the most positive of moments right now. Ignore the urge to consume tomorrows by living in the moment of today.

Heavens Rejoiced

I am saddened you consider yourself alone and worthless. I assure you, the Heavens rejoiced the day you were born. You are the hope of a magnificent life journey. You are needed in this world. You are here for a reason.

Pray for the arms of angels to carry you through rough waters. Seed love, goodwill, and peace within your soul. Be amazed at the healing powers of the Universe.

My friend, be remembered for your journey and good deeds. Show gratitude for your life and life lessons.

Shine brightly, my friend, for you are loved, and you will never be alone.

TENDRILS OF GOODNESS

Gifts of Kindness

Troubled you are at man's chosen destiny. Programming bombarded with negativity. Is there no space—on air or reality—for the goodness that still exists?

We are all floating amidst the darkness of lost souls. Look not to the dark but the glory of the whole. We have such potential. Turn your actions to the betterment for all.

Start small. Open a door. Simply say, *Hello*.

One kind word planted in the heart of another. See how it grows. Tendrils of goodness seeking God's Light.

Natural gifts of kindness are contagious. Infect mankind with the seed of kindness. The seed you plant today can alter the destiny of man tomorrow.

Kindness is free to give. Priceless to the receiver.

Life to the Fullest

I recognize your challenges. So much to do within the limits of an earthly lifetime. You require the speed and agility of a hummingbird.

Take care of your body. The spirit will follow. Nourishment and the leisure of the moment are required to maintain a tedious schedule.

Again you pause, disbelief forever creeping from the darkened caverns of fear.

Doubt will sacrifice your journey—are you willing to stop now? Think not. Just do. The more you learn, the faster the momentum will flow.

Judge not the obstacles in your earthly path. Have you not learned that those bumps are the most important lessons needed to bring you closest to God?

Look to your earthly obligations with peace. Joyfully live, work, and play.

Stop not. You've been gifted this lifetime.

Waste not. You've been gifted this lifetime.

Forever be joyful. Forever be kind and compassionate. Forever be the best, do the best, love the most, laugh the longest, live your life to the fullest. Forever.

This is your gift. Waste not.

Gifted Conversation

I long for the connections of our past. Happy times engaged in laughter and silliness.

Now we mirror that which was meant to facilitate.

Flat. Distant. Mechanical.

We worry of missed connections through beeping, ringing, and typed responses.

Let me see and feel the caverns of your soul.

Meet me. Speak to me. Allow me the privilege of seeing the furrows of your brow flex and accentuate excitement or sorrow.

Leave behind the texting and messaging. I do not care for that which you ate last night or which outfit you recently bought.

I care for you.

Are you well? Are you happy? What lessons of life have you mastered since we last spoke?

Words spoken, a rarity these days.

Were you not gifted with a tone that rings harmoniously with my soul?

Meet with me. Speak with me. Gift me conversation and the joy of your presence.

Time Gifted

Guilt is shared. Too much missed to mention. Too busy to notice. Lovely assortment of hues in variation. Simply, too busy.

Take the time. Time is what you have. Yours to manage or throw away. One precious moment stretched within itself can feel like a million. Slow your pace. Manage moments with observation.

Heed hectic schedules. Drama misplaced or created. Train yourself. Listen. Breathe. Time gifted today will be gone tomorrow. One moment. Stop now. Go outside or to a window. What joyful visual exchange has God gifted?

Negotiate the moment.

THOUGHTS INTO REALITY

Prayers Linked

I couldn't agree more. If thoughts were our reality, where would we be? If the warm days of summer lingered and there was tolerance for fall. To never lose power. And the house was always warm. If children were fed and nurtured. If kind acts replaced ignorance. If education required tolerance for all.

If mere intention gave life to amazing things.

Join me then. Let's try! Give intention. Create the most wondrous planet empty of strife. Love pouring from every heart. Prayers linked together. Goodwill. Encouragement. Understanding. Patience. Tolerance for the differences of worship, skin color, age, or nation.

Join me. Turn purest of intentions into reality.

LIFE GIFTED

Purity of Love

You are loved regardless the pace or place of your journey thus far. Regardless the circling behaviors that challenge that thought. You *are* loved.

A life gifted you hold in your hands. Turn away from the behaviors that hurt the soul and hinder the path. You *are* loved.

Look not back on where you have been. Look to this captured moment of thought and breath. Look to God's graces of which you are blessed.

You *are* loved for not what you hold in your hand or the roof above your head. You *are* loved not for your station in life or the family from which you come. You *are* loved for the purity of your soul.

Let not man nor circumstance dictate what you can be, where you can go, or the heights you can reach. For you *are* loved, supported, and blessed from this moment to the next.

A life gifted you hold in your hands. Waste not this captured moment. May you witness the unfolding of nature and feel the surge of God's love.

You *are* loved.

FORGIVENESS

Generosity Gifted

G enerosity gifted.
Forgiveness.
Simply said.

GOD STANDS READY

Fly with Intention

Willingly you cling. Afraid to let go. Timid in actions. Timid in life. Stagnant in a pool full of blessings. My friend, it is impossible to fly without intention.

Shed the cocoon. Spread your wings. Headway cannot be made without forward momentum. Let go and fly! Fear not the brief plummet before gaining speed. God stands ready to catch your fall. Trust in your abilities.

Fly, beautiful butterfly. Fly!

SADNESS CARRIED

Love Planted

I caught a glimpse of your sadness when together we last sat. Alone into the past you drifted. Staggering through intimate passages. Lost in a harvested field of cuttings and debris. Sifting through leftover emotional yields from life's challenges. Legs drawn to your chest. My friend, the field in which you sit needs to be planted.

God has graced you with many talents. Blessings abound. Grab onto my hand. Carry you I will until you can run on your own. Run to the abundance that waits. A life overwhelmingly full of joy and successes. Plant the seeds. Fill empty furrows with God's love. See not past yields but what *is* to come. Focus on the positives.

Give gratitude for you have been blessed. Given a new day, new dreams, and new chances at success. Run with the life God has gifted. Run, dear one, to plant sweet life chances.

WEIGHT OF THE WORLD

Life's Dilemmas

I worry for the schedule you keep. Daylight hours pass into night. Pulled this way and that. Dragged from your feet across nations. The weight of the world resting on fragile shoulders. Goals to reach. The head spinning. No rest . . . even with sleep.

How long can you carry this burden so great? Heart and soul never at rest. Worries for the world. Such a dark place in which we live.

Organize your desk. Organize your life. Put into compartments the things you can control. Sit quietly. The answers to life's questions will come when you slow down. The answers are there if only you will listen.

My friend, do what you can and release the rest to God. This planet will shine when shadows across the heart are unveiled. Your Light combines with mine. Together reflecting God's graces and blessings.

Be well. Sleep restfully. For you are God's angel and your love and tenderness are desperately needed.

PRAYER FOR A FRIEND

Peace and Harmony

May you find peace, safety, protection, joy, and love in all that you see and do.

May you live to behold beauty and miracles of many levels and degrees.

May anger and fear be replaced with love, understanding, and compassion.

May God guide you to peace and tranquility.

GOING HOME

Passage of Time

It comes for many reasons. Fragility. Susceptibility. Ravages of time or illness. The exterior no longer mirrors the interior.

When did it happen? Hopscotch yesterday. Footsteps carefully planted today. Time continues to slip through hands unrecognized. The body bends, swells, creaks, and groans.

It is the journey of life.

Hold tightly to remembrances of meadows laced with dew drops and butterflies. Remain young at heart. Remain strong in faith. Remain hardy in laughter. Proudly carry the knowledge learned to forgive and let go.

A promise God has gifted. When this journey concludes, another begins.

GOD WILL FILL THE VOID

Exterior Wrap

I don't know where to begin. Love you, I do, with all my heart. Concern for your health. No longer capable of play. You squander precious life moments imprisoned within yourself. Do you look to fill your belly or the void of your life?

Void there need not be. So much living if you could only see. It's not the exterior wrap. It's your health and mental well-being. You're vital in the collection of the whole. You have a purpose. Soul journey and life goals. Look to God to fill the emptiness.

If journey's end were to be announced, would you wish for this as your final existence? Or would you rather join hands with me? We'll puddle jump and skip. Play as adults, like when we were kids.

Heavenly blessed you are. To be whom you are in this time and place. Fill the void in your life with God's grace. Be healthy. Be happy. You are vital in the collection of the whole. The whole of humanity. Your existence makes a difference.

GOD NOT GLORY

Soaring and Searching

You are a hawk. Soaring . . . searching. Perched high in the midst of a storm. Experiencing the moment instead of controlling it.

You are a hawk. Soaring . . . searching. Dreams laced with wisdom. Gifted from a higher source. Words carefully placed. Timing and images blended together. Expending energy. Extending yourself. Secure with the knowledge good deeds are contagious.

Reminder needed. Gratefully received. Look to God and not glory when perched high in the midst of a storm. Spread compassion. Together we can turn this world around.

DEPTHS OF DEPRESSION

Inner Strength Emerged

Depression is the equalizer. It takes souls hostage regardless of social or ethnic status. It comes forth hidden under the cloak of fear.

Fear of the unknown. Fear of the unfamiliar. Fear of solitude. Fear of loss.

You danced with fear . . . then depression. Drapes drawn, lights out . . . you sat in darkness. Depression and fear thrive in darkness. For in darkness you are blinded to what was, what is, and what will come.

So you sat. Alone. Feeding fear. Feeding depression.

But you were never alone. For the Universe embraced you, offering comfort within Earth Mother's rocking motion. Morning to night, morning to night, morning to night.

Still blinded, you cried, *Why have all forsaken me?* Friends, loved deeply, turned and disappeared leaving shadows of mere memories haunting your daily existence. *Why?* Did you not love enough?

You begged to return to the arms of your Creator. And then. . . .

The faintest Light began to emerge. Your Light. Giving yourself to the Universe, you asked to be healed. With your head planted upon the bosom of Earth Mother, you grounded yourself within her strength. You awoke to the unfolding of your soul, and your inner strength emerged.

A miracle was bestowed upon you. Love cascading in a blanket of heavenly light, lifted the darkness. The Universe ushered you to peace and tranquility. Peace replaced sorrow. Knowing replaced ignorance. Love and forgiveness filled the empty caverns of your heart.

You are of God's Light.

RESTLESSLY PACE

Heavenly Path

I watch as you restlessly pace. A magnitude of changes from within that overflow about. You've become productive, no longer consumed with self-doubt. Filling your mind with knowledge. Filling your pad with thoughts.

Be creative. Open the shade. Let in the Light. Awaken the sleeping souls. Reach for the stars whilst traversing along *your* most upward path.

Peace through Faith

I am so sorry to hear of your newest challenge. Life certainly twists and turns unexpectedly. My words cannot relieve your painful suffering. Your peace will come through faith.

You are not alone. You are not alone through your restless nights and exhausting days. Look, my friend, for the sprig of hope and God's Light that shines in the darkest moments.

Prayers will find their way to you through God's love and comfort.

FATIGUED AND WEARY

God's Hand

Fatigued and weary you seem. Societal standards. Unrealistic demands. When will you have enough? When will you be enough? Time ticks on. The calendar changes.

My dear friend, there's more to life than acquisitions. Acquisitions of title. Acquisitions physical in nature. There are acquisitions of the heart. Gather heartfelt connections. The abundance you already possess.

Put for yourself a goal in mind. A goal to play at life. Think back to childhood games. Use of the imagination. Creation. Works of art. Masterpieces in a child's eye. Songs sung loudly and carefree. Think back to the joy of these experiences. Live your life through a child's eyes. Find the child within that still exists. The child of faith. Close to God. Visions laced with innocence.

Like an old photograph, remember play. Running through fields. Splashing through puddles. Fingers painting. Toes wiggling. Giggling.

Rest your weariness. Release the demands and standards for just ten minutes and play. No guarantee for tomorrow. Time ticks on. The calendar changes.

CYCLE OF ADDICTION

Unite in Prayer

Stop blaming. Drastic action required. Cemeteries overly populated with innocents. Children and adults of all ages caught off guard. Worrisome burden you carry for your own. How could this be? Not yours . . . wedged in the cycle and fall of addiction. Wearing a camouflaged haze of a toughened exterior. Beneath the cries from a struggling soul. Weeping for lack of strength and insight. The lost vision of self-worth. Unacquainted with grace. Losing sight of potential. Diming of their Light.

Hide not behind the scrutiny of others. Reach out. Build a network of protective energy. Unity required to aid through the nightmarish reality of drugs and alcohol. Parents, teachers, preachers, speakers, families, and friends unite in prayer. Unite in a call for an end to addictions. Hold tight against the storm. Seek solace as a whole instead of alone.

Encourage you may, recognizing their grace. But sit not blinded to your own. The power you hold as a person, parent, or friend. The power of prayer. Thank God for assisting through life's stumbles and falls. Thank God for life.

Drastic action required. Unity of prayers. Solace as a whole instead of alone.

LIFE SUSPENDED

Technology

You stand in the shadows of invisibility. Covered by a cloak of technology. Reading. Watching. Justifying. Spewing. Raging from within at the audacity of others. How dare they carry on! How dare they live their lives as though nothing has happened!

My friend, it is you that carries the torch lighted. You that brings forth the past. It is you that scans for the next social-media posting.

But what of your life? Your decisions? What of the actions you sent forth to the Universe before things unfolded?

It is time to let go.

Put to rest the magnifying glass you carry in your hip pocket. Examine your own intentions before examining the actions of others.

There are no guarantees to the length of stay on this planet. Life can be suspended without notice.

It is your life that is being wasted.

Release the burdensome acts of aggression. Create space in your life for new relationships and paths to travel. Leave to the side the finger-pointing intentions. Fill your heart and life with love, compassion, and forgiveness. Fill your life with meaning. You were put here for a reason.

Majestically Speaking

How beautiful is this place called home. Majestically speaking of spaces cultivated or freely roamed. River's flow running opposite conventional currents. Hot lavender sunrise hues to sunsets yellow-orange infused. My friend, take a moment. Reflect from your heart-place on home.

Taken so often for granted. Glory at the doorstep. Travel gently. Don't trample. For in all her splendor, Earth Mother will suffer.

Openly weep. For when you look, you will truly see the hand of God on every plant, animal, and tree. Every rock, crevasse, and grain of sand. Every person around the planet and back around again.

How beautiful is this place called home. Set your clock. Make the appointment. Visit tonight's sunset.

ADRENALINE PACE

Precious Life Cargo

So quickly you sprint. Adrenaline pace. Rushing a dead-ended ladder instead of taking your time. So eager to go, go, go. My friend, you've lost the moment and precious life cargo.

The drills of life are intended to be pleasant. To what direction is it from which you run? Climbing corporate ladders or avoidance of the should-have-done. What of enjoying the moment and allowing life to unfold. Releasing the worries of what's to come.

Follow your heart in the being of the moment. Focus on God's blessings. The ladder to rush is a spiritual one.

GOD'S GIFTED BREATH

Faith

Fear lifts its ugly head. Warnings run along your spine. Your stomach knots. You drop that which you hold in your hands. Dreams and forward movement left behind.

What is it that lurks in the shadows? Fear of secrets told? Fear of the unknown? Fear of abandonment? Fear of not measuring up? Fear of success?

Face that which is feared the most. Child of God, you stand not alone. What secrets are there that cannot be told? For God already knows your shadowed past inside and out. Success is but one step ahead. One foot forward. The other will follow.

My friend, God has gifted you breath. Promises of sunrises and sunsets. Regardless of the past paths taken.

Hold onto your faith. Hold on to God's hand. God has not given up, dear one. Steady on your feet. One foot forward. The other will follow.

Life with God is life without fear.

RAMBLING ON

Listening Heart

Sometimes I am amazed by my self-centeredness. Forgive me. Rambling on of things that carry little importance instead of asking the weighty questions. What good graces have you encountered today? How is your heart? Heavy or carefree? How are *you*, my friend?

So eager are you to greet each day. Sun rising as well as your spirits. Welcoming life with warm embraces. Joyfully expressing gratitude to God for blessings transparent and hidden.

Oh, what wonderful lessons have I to learn if only I would listen.

So . . . now clear-headed and balanced within myself, let me ask of you. Listen I will with my heart as well as my ears.

How are you, my dear friend?

POWER TO SWAY

Live Humble

We each possess the power to sway. For political agendas or personal reasons. Through words and actions. When life offers a choice, simply sway Divine. Justification never required. For justification follows actions taken below the belt.

Excuse me. For always there will exist the option of action of the highest intention. Let go of the ego-laden choices backed by excuses. Simply live your life humble in God's graces.

Pray for others. Recognize gifts granted. Offer compassion and forgiveness. Live in God's Light. Live by example. When living a life full of grace, no explanation is ever required.

EMOTIONAL SUFFERING

Finding God's Light

You were well-meaning and compassionate. Heart in the right place. Painfully witnessing the emotional suffering. Hurriedly rushing to make things right. Interceding on their behalf.

Sometimes the rough spots come for a reason.

Times there will be when assistance should be granted. But there are times when knowledge is gained through experience. The knowledge graced when open to God's Light. Offer compassion, love, and encouragement by allowing *them* to fix their problems.

Deny them not the satisfaction of pride in a new path taken . . . or of finding God along the way.

A Heart Consumed

From my heart to yours. Embracing with verse. Distaste written in the furrows of your face. Angry at life. Withered in self-pity. Dehydrated within self-consumed slumber. Back turned from the well of good works. My friend, gently stir from your confrontational sleep.

Dramatically change the direction of concern. From you to another. Feel the well of compassion fill in your sacred heart-place. Fill the furrows of your heart with Light. Anger will cease to exist with a heart consumed in peace.

Drink freely from the well of compassion. Set free good deeds. When giving gratitude near the end of day's light . . . ask of yourself. How far have your good deeds traveled today? To what extent have you cradled and consoled collapsed silhouettes in the field of life? Remembering always it is of our positive interaction with the world around us that brings peace. Peace in spirit. Peace with Earth Mother. Peace braided with compassion.

Rest well, my friend. Feel my heart wrapped about yours. May your well of good deeds and compassion run free.

GOD'S VOICE

Through the Wind

Remember . . . we are never alone. God is always with us. His voice comes to us in many different ways.

From the cry of a baby to the roar of a wave. From a tear of hope to a warm embrace. It's carried by the wind from a homeless soul's lips to a rich man's fitful sleep.

God's voice runs through our veins.

Cleaner Planet

Tragic it is. So much waste. Waste of time. Waste of money. Waste of food. Waste of resources. Whilst empty bellies and strife is felt by the many. Cascading the globe.

One person can make the difference. Positive change is contagious to the whole. Shake free of the selfishness that keeps you idling on low.

Start small.

Empty your trash can of unnecessary debris. Compost. Recycle. Switch to natural and renewable energy.

Support organizations that feed. Support organizations that offer a bed and hot meal. Support organizations that work for the whole, the many, and not the CEOs.

With ease the transition can be made when gifting to others. A cleaner planet. Children no longer left unfed.

We walk this journey together. Linked by our hearts and breath. We are of the same Father.

Look today not at what you need, but what can you do for another.

PROSPERITY OF POWER

Richness of Heart

Wealth is accessible in many forms. Many are consumed with treasures of the dollar. Others with the prosperity of power. Political and corporate sovereigns gorge themselves on the power of the dollar. My friend, wealth need not be tangible. The true gem of existence is the richness of heart.

True wealth is a day spent in prayer. Offering gratitude for blessings of simplicity and peace. True wealth is witnessing a sunrise or putting a sunset to sleep. True wealth is having enough to share. Sharing of oneself. When possible, sharing a dollar. True wealth is the treasure carried within. Knowledge of God's love. True wealth is the richness of heart.

My dear friend, I wish you a life full of compassion. A life spent living each moment. A life in service to humanity and Earth Mother. A life simple and peaceful. I wish for you the richness of heart.

Lift the Spirits of Others

Saint you are not . . . that is correct. But would your tender messages hold the same value negate your suffering and life lessons? For it is through your humanness that *we* connect.

Struggle you do. Normal, I would say. Fleeing moments resisting judgment of others. Judgement of yourself. It's what you do with those moments that sets you apart from your past.

When lacing compassion against yourself, an easier place you will find. Blending a mixture of understandings of where you are and where *we* go together as a human race.

Be the best. Happiest. Kindest. You will lessen the struggles within yourself. You will lift the spirits of others through your humanness.

Gratitude Gifted

It happens so easily. I'm guilty as well. Straight-jacketed within yourself. You fail to acknowledge the merit of others. Good deeds either unseen or forgotten.

Too busy or too tired.

To each we owe kind and considerate words. Soft-spoken well wishes. Gratitude unfolded. Everyday niceties. Smiles and actions no longer taken for granted.

When was the last time you acknowledged a stranger?

Good day and God bless! Words gently plucked and stroked play like music to their soul.

I appreciate your efforts. Thanks to your mother . . . she raised you well. Encourage the youth. Troubled times for them. Recognize success. Giving a boost for the seventh generation to come.

Open your eyes. Take a deep breath. Be never too busy nor too tired to recognize the greatness in a friend.

Personal Decisions

What's happened to you? Strong and confident once you were. Now caught in the cycle of perpetual flight. Fleeing from pleasures and lessons of life. Squandering abilities on second guesses and don't knows. Unsteady and off-balanced.

Beware of stealers of time. Stealers of talent. Stealers of decisions. Stealing your life. Guised as a well-wisher, a know-more, and smarter-than-you. Inciting fear for the unknown. Stealing your right to stand strong. Stealing your sense of standing on your own.

The ingredients for self-approval and self-worth are easily developed. Accept yourself for all that is good and all that is not. Less than better decisions are easily corrected. Listen to your heart and not your head.

Sometimes in life the best lessons are difficult. Reflection required and a fresh start.

Follow your instincts instead of the demands of another. Stretch your abilities. Take a few chances. You'll find exactly where your talents lie. So what if you fall. You can always get up and stand tall.

ONE DAY AT A TIME

Seek Strength

I remember you as an innocent youth, trying your hand at many things.

Somewhere . . . somehow, life has gotten muddled, and your outlook is hazy.

You whittle away hours wallowing in despair, caught in a cycle without a beginning or end.

What holds you frozen in your stride?

The life clock continues to tick.

Acquaintances of your youth, now successful and distant, are nothing more than a mere memory—like your dreams and life expectations. Why them and not you? Did you not yearn for the same things? Have you not held dreams within your heart?

And so, you continue the cycle. Unable to start. Unable to stop. You move through life at the pace of a snail, while life continues its spin regardless your momentum.

Where's the strength of the wondering child? The head-strong youth, ready for life and all of life's rewards.

I see your potential. But, alas, my hands are tied. It is your journey.

Wake up, dear one. Awake from your earthly nightmare. Take on life one day at a time. Take effort. Take God.

Stop the ego's barrage of self-deprecating behavior. If victim is what you seek, then victim you shall be. Seek strength. Seek miracles. Seek the energy to *see* the moment and carry that momentum to the next. Seek God.

LET GO OF THE PAST

Peace

I helplessly watch as you waste a lifetime seeking that which will never come.

Approval.

Confirmation.

Love from those now departed.

You seek that which was never realized. Adulthood spent tending the leftovers of your youth. You tend their possessions better than your parents tended you.

Matters not how the details of your life are manipulated and misconstrued, past or present. You know who you are. If you don't, let me help you.

You are a child of God.

Your parents were merely your earthly guardians. Job done well or not; it takes not away from you. Child of God. Beautiful and cherished you have always been.

Hold not onto that which will never come. The disappointments of your upbringing will not be sufficed through things—but through actions. Your actions.

Let go of the past. Tend to the child within. Seek peace in your heart. Dance carefree to the songs of the wind. Release the urge to hold onto things of the past. Release kindness to others. Release kindness to yourself.

You are a child of God. Beautiful and cherished you have always been.

Comfort through Prayer

I am sorry for your loss.

You carry the sorrow and tears to fill the depths of a million oceans.

Reach to hold your hand—help I cannot. Cry with you, lament a lifetime's of what-ifs—help I cannot.

Take your sorrow to God. Seek comfort with Him.

LOSS OF A PERFECT DAY

Simple Joys of Youth

It rained today. So sad were you for the intrusion into your desire for a perfect day.

Stop.

Look within. Look out. Were not the soft hues of darkening clouds glorious? Was not the fresh drink of water released to the earth a miracle? Look not to God's miracle with negative connotations. Look to the miracle with the wonder and excitement of a child. Look for the miracle of rain for that which it is—a blessing.

Forget the tedious restrictions of maturity that bind you indoors. Don the play clothes of youth. Puddle jump in God's miracle. Puddle jump until the child within remembers. Forget not the simple joys of your youth. Get wet. Get muddy. Play.

Then thank God for the beautiful day.

VIOLENCE AND DRAMA

Prayers to the Universe

We share the same aversion to news events, pop star outfits, and reality show hits. Drama unnecessarily geared sensational. Our world writes a story of its own. Violence and drama on every page.

What if attention was not paid to negatives? Gifting them back from where they came.

What if more important were things of a positive nature? Lifting the spirits of the suffering through actions and words of encouragement. Sending prayers to the Universe.

Imagine being tuned-in to grand discoveries aiding humankind. Applauding challenges overcome. Documentaries on the goodness still prevalent in the peoples of the world. What of the day-to-day miracles taken for granted? The butterfly drying flawlessly formed wings. A baby's first breath. A flower in bloom.

When the news is full of positives, I'll tune back in. Until then, I'll continue to focus on the good whilst ignoring the rest.

Preacher Speaker Writer Teacher

You have the heart of a lion. Strong and protective. Fearless you are of misinterpretations and malice.

You are not a reckless runner of companies. You *are* the preacher, speaker, writer, and teacher. You are gifted and blessed with a sensitivity to man.

Worry not who is listening. Your words and actions laced with grace will find their proper place.

Your purest intentions *will* translate.

BURDENS DRAGGED

Reach for the Light

Hopelessly you cling. Final bloom closing. Delicate leaves downward nodding. Roots wrapped about dirt and waste. A once beautiful flower sadly wilts in the harshness of life. Nurturing sorely needed. My friend, reach for the Heavens. Feed on God's Light.

Spread your roots and draw from Earth Mother. Look not to waste. Look to God for relief. Relief of burdens dragged through canyons of emptiness. Relief of painful memories. Let God nurture and lift your soul.

Fill your heart with buds of hope, compassion, direction, and positive intentions. Turn towards the Light. You are here for a reason. Blossom. Bloom. Reach for God's Light.

SERVICE TO HUMANITY

United through Love

Perplexed you seem to be with weighted situations. The dilemma of intersecting crosswalks of life. When the opportunity arises to pick a direction—choose that of a higher calling.

Service to humanity.

Service of kinship, compassion, the offering of time. Reaching out. Lifting up suffering souls. Kind words spoken. Generous tokens. Spreading yourself beyond your four walls.

You walk this path not alone, but with brothers and sisters of all nations and religions. United through tough times and a love of God.

Expand your path through prayerful interaction. Across land and waters. Reach out in prayer to other nations.

Positive intentions lift the vibration for all.

Be a service to humanity. Offer of yourself beyond your four walls.

Each Person has Their Place

So testy and agitated you are of late. Impatient and belittling of strangers and friends. Attitude towards choices *they make*. How to talk, walk, dress, and eat. So much time wasted questioning and judging the actions and decisions of others. Stop trying to remold them. Allow for dignity in differences.

Look to what you deem as a fault, but more as a gift from God. Uniqueness is His specialty. Look closely at the Universe. Are we not as different as garden arrangements?

Needed are procrastinating dreamers to see life through visions. Needed are take-charge doers birthing the visions into actions. Needed are nitpicking detailers delivering the actions to fruition. Needed are kind-hearted souls bridging the gap.

Balancing energies is embracing humanity. Each person on this planet has their place. Thanks to God—we are all *not* the same. Look to the differences with joy and compassion. Pick up the slack and honor their gift as well as your own.

Dream. Do. Think. Connect. It will be for the greater good of all.

Feeding on Fear and Distrust

It comes with many labels. The darkness behind dead-ended eyes. Bone-chilling coldness. The shadow that lurks in the absence of God's Light.

Offer no energy for it feeds on fear and distrust.

Overpower the negatives of television and social media. Overpower the negatives in your day-to-day life. Bring balance to thought and personal connections in a positive nature. Look not to the darkness of situations or people—but to the Light.

Shine brightly, my friend. For the shadow cannot exist in full Light.

THINGS LEFT UNSAID

Dearly Loved

I was amiss. Shaded view from which I sit. Excuses there are none. For news of your health brought such concern. Valued friendship leaves little room for things left unsaid and undone.

My apology stands in front. Closely behind follow riveted decisions. Consideration for health and happiness of one so dearly loved. Gratitude for our friendship. Thinking and feeling are not enough. Need to know of your status on a regular basis. Four days in the hospital—I would have brought flowers.

So with that said, be assured. Dearly you are loved. Welcome are conversations and time privately spent. Please stay in touch.

Blessings to you of spring tulips and good health. You are loved.

KEY TO THE UNIVERSE

Sending Love

Too painful to view. Photographs from another life. Forever you are as when I saw you last. Reminded I am of time. Mind's eye shut. Too painful to view. Mementos stacked and organized. Hidden amongst pages of tear-stained diaries.

You hold in your heart the key to the Universe. Open the door to forgiveness. Open the door to memories. Unlock the goodness carried within. Love's tugging reminder of time spent together.

Love, dear one. The continuation of energy in one form to another. Transcending distance, time, and the passing of life.

Wherever you are please know it is love I send.

Refuge in God's Blessings

Overcoming. A tribute to human suffering. Overcoming despair, heartache, sorrow, and physical challenges. Overcoming hunger, racism, war, and hatred. Overcoming self-inflicted hurdles along life's path.

You are stronger than you think. Held in the palm of your hand is the power of the Universe. Power to overcome. If only you have faith.

Faith in yourself as an individual and faith in the human race. Take refuge in God's blessings, for gifted within is the power to overcome.

ACCEPTANCE OF ALL

Integrity of the Whole

Families are not held together by the one but by the integrity of the whole. Need for compassion goes beyond four walls.

Teach your children the unity of souls. Teach discipline of the mind to follow the heart instead of the dollar. Importance there is to make a living. Modern conveniences should not be denied. But in the race to provide neglect not the nurturing of prayer, commonality, and grace. Acceptance of all peoples, religions, and nations.

The integrity of your home will then flow to the integrity of the whole.

SMOLDERING ASH

Wounds of the Heart

You battle within yourself. One part is wanting and the other shut off. Heatedly lashing and thrashing all the goodness that lay in your lap. Blinded by anger. Self-absorbed in feeding the wounds of the heart. Barely visible is the smoldering ash of your Light.

Go back in time. To a happier place. Freely playing in God's Light. Tender sunshine kisses. Nature beneath your feet. Joyfully giving of yourself and talents.

Wage war no longer. Put down your shield. Open yourself gently to the healing power of God. Giving your heart and talents is a blessing in disguise. For in the moment of giving it is not possible to be absorbed in yourself.

PASSING OF A FRIEND

Legacy Continuance

Together we weep for the loss of a friend. Good person. Long life. Wrapped now in the arms of an angel ascending toward Heaven.

Look not to your place of dwelling amongst dust-laden trinkets for healing. A lifetime boxed and sealed. Look to your heart for the most valuable possessions. Memories that can't be traded. Good deeds and kind gestures. Laughter. Love of life. Love of family. Strong through strife. In your heart carefully tend the remnants and legacy of that passion.

Shoulder to shoulder in a line across this great nation. Reaching to Heaven and beyond. One action and intention remembered from every soul our friend encountered. A smile. A gesture. A joke timely placed. A hug. Bacon and eggs for breakfast. Grab hands with the person closest in line. Share stories. Remembrances. Listen and feel the distance of our friend's reaching.

Lay to rest the great warrior and child of God. But rest not our friend's far-reaching passion for life.

ABANDONED

Forgiveness Granted

May I call you *friend*? Recognize your energy—I do not. Approach me in my dreams. Let me feel you in my heart. Questions to ask. Answers untold. Learning to let go.

Do you think of me now that you are in Heaven?

Let me tell you of how I turned out.

Alone, I grew through uncertainties. Abandoned at the beginning of life's journey. Left to my own devices. Compassionate and good . . . I have tried to be. Sensitive to suffering.

Angry at you I have never been . . . walked in your shoes I have not. Confused perhaps for your choice of destiny. Trailing off. Loving and watching a slew of new innocents through their life journey of firsts.

But wasn't I your first?

Ask you I will when your heart energy is near. Long to hold me when I was young, did you not?

When my Earth walk finally comes to an end. As I near Heaven's gate. Please, don't miss my first step through. Be there please for an eternity to embrace my energy with yours. I look forward to meeting you.

GIFTED MIRACLES

Burdens Faced

I know this place of which you speak. Blanketed under the fight
to merely exist. Challenges around every corner. Nothing
gifted. Never easy.

My friend, more wrong you could not be. For each breath
is a gifted miracle.

No guarantees for this walk we take. Not for the length of
time or ease of things. It is the attitude in which the energy
might be better placed. Look at where you are. Imagine where
you would like to be. Give gratitude for the stumbles and jogs
along the way. You have been blessed.

When days seem overwhelming . . . then to the moment you
should go. In this moment of moments that make your day, look
to the gratitude of heart. Gratitude for breath. A sunrise. Sunset.
One more step in God's graces.

Challenges there will always be. Face them with dignity and
grace. Allow your Light to shine.

BALLERINA STANCE

Wave of Indecision

So carefully you pose in ballerina stance. Testing the waters until a wave of indecision sets you back. To reach for the stars, first you must leap. Leap from the murky shore of disbelief. Walk flat-footed to waters deep. Close your eyes to foggy inhibitions. Follow faith.

Faith in God. Faith in yourself. Not to say you won't get knocked from your feet. Stand back up. Face the deep. Smile to yourself. You are so much stronger than you think.

Going the distance requires God's grace and faith in yourself. There's much more to life. There's much more to you. Leap, my friend. Leap.

PERSONAL DISASTER

God Held Your Hand

Sorry for your loss. Escaped in your nightclothes. Personal disaster. God held your hand. Inconvenience monumental. Earthly treasures relinquished to dust.

Critical to value that which you hold. Greater gifts will come to pass. Awareness of that which is important . . . life itself.

Rebuild your tomorrows. The grandeur of life imposed. Lost trinkets and mementos replaced.

Forget not gratitude through troublesome delays. Life in perspective. Remembrances of that which is sacred and that which can be changed. Daily acknowledgments of guidance gifted and God holding your hand.

MEDIOCRE

Failure to Shine

Mediocre. Sad definition. Sad existence. For when settling for mediocre, you fail to shine. Challenge yourself in all aspects of life. Be known and remembered for your Light. Child of God, you were put here for a reason. Shared acts of kindness congeal.

Life was gifted as a joyful experience. Challenge yourself. Sit with yourself. Have you done all you can do? Gifted your time? Shared of yourself and talents? Extended beyond a mediocre life?

God's blessings you carry. Meant to be shared. Not selfishly harvested and vaulted away. Shine, dear one. Shine in God's Light.

Be the best. Do the best. Give of yourself. Shine.

Live not a mediocre life. Live in God's Light.

TRUST FAITH GOD

Soar

Rocky trails color the hills with uncertainty. Fragile is your self-esteem. Fear of miss-stepped intentions. After all, you may fall—or you may soar!

Close your eyes to the obstacles and focus on the goals. Life is a series of bumps and plummets. Wrap fear in a linen handkerchief. Place it in your front pocket. Release it as needed when personal safety is involved. The rest of life's uncertainty is meant to be unknown.

Trust. Faith. God. Soar.

Live life to its fullest. Let go of the fears that hold you in place. Release your fears to God—and soar!

SHARDS OF NOTHINGNESS

Hold onto God

You carry a heart full of despair. Pacing, projecting what ifs, protecting what is. So much effort wasted wrapping yourself around things. Insignificant shards of nothingness to the world. Cherished smatterings of treasures to you.

Fearful of discovery are you. Is it not that you wish to look outward? Is it not you fear to look inward? Recognizing the emptiness. A heart filled not with Light or dark. Filled with nothingness.

So you hoard. You hoard many things. Bad memories, lost dreams, bits and pieces of nothingness that can serve of no benefit to your soul.

You are caught in the rush of *holding*.

There is something you can hold which will not block your Light. Hold God. Hold tightly.

Let go of the insignificant earthy possessions. Clean up, clean out. Fill the emptiness of your life and heart with God's love. Tear down the blinds that close off Light. Tear down the blocks surrounding your heart. You are meant to feel God's warmth cascading upon your face. You are meant to feel. You are meant to shine.

Take God into your heart. Look to what is truly important and let go of the rest. Let Light shine through your windows. Let Light shine within your heart. Fill the emptiness of your life with His Light.

WEIGHT OF THE PAST

God's Graces

So heavily you step. Around your neck a serpent rests. Heavily coiled. Tightly wrapped. Pressing on hunched shoulders the weight of your past. My friend, let go of the burden so heartbreakingly toted. Let go.

Start now in this moment. Look not back but forward. That was then. You are now. Shed the skin of the past. Emerge newly formed. Child of God, you carry within the faith to move mountains. Move yourself. Move forward. Let go. Release the weight so tightly wrapped. Release to God.

Choices and paths shall always remain. Reach high. Follow God's Light. A future awaits. Bright and promising. Layered in God's graces. Your future . . . not the past. Walk upright. Reach high. Release your suffering to God in this moment of time, and never look back.

HUMBLENESS

In Light

Impatient we are as a whole. Wishing. Wanting. Reaching for earthly assets. Things of structure with which to hold.

What if the greatest of assets comes from selfless actions? Generosity towards others and Earth Mother. Generosity of love, affection, and attention. Generosity of time and dollar.

Selfless interactions and actions are the grandest to behold. Carried in the heart. Passed from soul to soul. Easing the difficult passage of life or circumstance.

Fill your moments lifting, helping, loving, and interacting with others. Reach for God's Light in all that you do. Things of structure will fall into place when you trust in God's love and follow His Light. You are here for a reason. Leave each step better than the last taken.

APATHY NOT PERMITTED

United We Walk

United we walk through life gifted. Light of God shines regardless of location. Raising awareness of hope and peace through prayerful exchange beyond oceans and mountain ranges. Your brothers are your brothers. Your sisters are your sisters. Reach out through your heart-place. Your prayer united with mine *can* make a difference.

Apathy not permitted. For we walk not alone in single file. My steps follow another. Perhaps yours in mine. We are united in sorrow and compassion. It is an obligation on this Earth walk to carry each other. An obligation that no one be left behind.

Pray for yourself. Pray for each other. Pray for joyful recognition of this glorious life gifted. Unite in compassion.

HARSHNESS OF YOU

Emotional Voice

I struggle with the harshness of you. Caught in the thrashing and scratching for an emotional voice. When all that is needed is compassion and allowance of time. Time for the unfolding of situations. Sanctioning the winds of today to send away yesterday's unrest.

Storms pass.

Instead, you covet unsettled thoughts. Reject conversations that cleanse. Deny heartfelt requests.

My friend, let go of the harshness that ravages your life. Settle disturbances without hurtful thoughts or actions, for they all circle back. Allow love in your life. Rock with the flow of time.

Go to your heart-place. Leave behind the ego and rage. Leave behind the war of thoughts that circle. Open your heart to a fresh start, like that of a gifted sunrise.

JOURNEY NEVER ENDING

Mourn not for Me

Mourn not for me at the end of my journey. For when it comes to the end of my time, I'll say goodbye with gratitude given. Sunsets, love, peace, and joy. Lessons of life and awakening unfolded. For visions beyond myself. Linking to humanity. Forgiveness through the eyes of compassion.

Mourn not for me at the end of my journey. For my journey will be never-ending. Promise I have from God. Life continues. Be it through the gifts left behind or transference of energy to the beyond.

Mourn not for yourself. For I am here. Tenderly ensuring love be not forgotten. My dearest one, so close to my heart. Live each day moment-to-moment. Dwell not on the past or worrisome tomorrows. Live full and well. Live life in peace within yourself. Life with the joy of a child. Happy to wake each gifted day.

Mourn not for me. Give gratitude. For friendship and love transcend the passage of time.

SPIDER'S WEB

Leap of Faith

There is a natural ebbing of life. Like the spindle of a spider's web. Enticing and connecting peoples and events. An intertwining maze of shared thoughts or experiences.

The question you must ask when partnered with honesty . . . *to which spindle are you caught?* The spindle of unrelenting thoughts and memories? Unhealthy relationships? Wanting for more? Jealousy? Selfishness? What keeps you stuck? Fear of letting go of unhealthy behavior or addictions—to people or things? You pass through life holding. Unable to jump free. Look to the web of your life. What sits waiting to devour peace, practicality, good deeds, and success?

My friend, keep your eyes closed if needed. Simply release.

Release tenderly. Open handed. Open-hearted. Let go of the web from which you are caught. With closed eyes and open heart—simply release. Child of God, you were meant to fly. Soar from the grip that keeps you from God. Soar from the grip that keeps you from peace. Soar from the grip of helpless. Take action. Take God.

The world awaits the fullness of you. Radiantly beautiful. Full of Light. Carry within a shield of strength, knowledge, goodness, and devotion. Carry within the love for yourself and the belief in your goodness—simply release.

Unity of Hearts

There is a better way. Better than cut-throat commerce and self-imposed solitude. There is a better way. Better than all-for-one and you're-on-your-own. There is a better way.

Better might be living in peace through the unity of hearts. Trading and bartering in a village of sustainability. Compassion gifted free of charge. Acknowledgment of neighbors near and far. Gifting your talents. Helping a friend.

Better than living within the eye-of-self is extending your hands, talents, prayers, and gifts. We are of the same breath. Child of God, find the village and give of yourself.

CONFRONTED MALICIOUSLY

Refuge in God's Blessings

Easy it is to veer. Drawn from peaceful solitude when confronted maliciously. Unkind words and actions strewed about. Sources of limited intelligence and classless intentions. Waver not, dear one. The reflection of their ugliness is carried across their heart.

Do not give credence to their actions or allow it to shape your reality. For an ocean of benevolence, unfamiliar to them, reigns in your heart. Seek refuge in blessings of home and friends. Your home is the manna that feeds your soul with the joy and wonders of nature. Gratitude for messages prevail. Firmly planted upon Earth Mother's soil, you shall remain.

Pity you should carry for the darkness of their soul. Compassion you should gift. Their words and actions carry strong to the crowd, but their reality is oneness.

Veer back, dear one, to the straight and upward path. Child of God, spreading good graces. Protected you are in the grand scheme of things. Sunrise to sunset. Sunrise to sunset. Within the four walls of your home and across great nations.

My friend, let not one unkind word or gesture veer you from your heavenly path. Remain grateful and patient, even when confronted with ignorance and malice. Let their actions be worn upon their face and burden their soul. Always there will be negative energy. Let it pass to the depths of the unknown.

RIVER BANK OF LONELINESS

Experience Life

If only I could embrace you with words. I see the blankness of your gaze. Open doors to nothingness. Your heart feels as empty as your house. You tread life's shore, tiptoeing amongst the rocks and boulders of emotion. A break wall in place protecting the heart's treasures.

Why do you wallow along the riverbank of loneliness? Afraid to swim to deep waters. Open your eyes. Try, once again, to experience the vast depths of life.

How can one so innocent and pure in love see blankness? Open your heart. Feel His love. Regardless of relationships that come and go. Loved ones distanced by miles or emotions. You are never alone. God is always at your side.

All you have to do is allow yourself to see the Light.

CHILD OF GOD

Beauty in Dissimilarity

I recognize the forced smile. Struggle with your image—it is clear to me. Envy for that which is deemed attractive. Fantasizing that smaller size or different hairstyle. Society focuses on celebrity makeovers and diet plans. Forgotten is recognition of beauty in dissimilarity.

A prayer that these words mend your perceived reality.

You are unique. One of a kind. Beautiful in your own right. God created *you*. He doesn't make junk. You are who you were intended to be. Different from all others. My friend, you are blindingly beautiful in my eyes and His as well. A child of God created from love. Radiant in His Light. Unique in appearance as a sunset sky.

Let the Light within outshine your misconceptions. You are beautiful. Glorious. Loved. Cherished. One of a kind. A dazzling beacon of radiant Light.

Matching exteriors are not what matters.

CLOVER TO BUTTERCUPS

Beauty in All

L et not one day pass without high expectations. Expectations that moments of wonder, excitement, and pleasure will fill your day. Then, give thanks when those expectations are met.

Spread your wings as a tender butterfly on its virgin flight. Look and see what is before your very eyes.

Pigeons and songbirds littering city fences and rooftops coo and majestically sing. Clover and buttercups burst from the soil in contrasting colors along sidewalks and across farmers' fields. Children, different as buttercups and clover, spread God's Light in innocent and glorious play.

Warm smiles, well wishes, and embraces from forged friendships are not the necessities of life. But as a communal existence, please remember, we are all the same breath. The breath of the Father.

Waste not one moment. Look for the beauty. Look for what is wonderful, exciting, and pleasurable in all that you do. In all of your travels, and with all of God's creations.

We are all the same breath. From pigeons to songbirds, clover to buttercups, to the children of many colors and to the different songs they sing—there is such beauty.

DIFFERENT TO SOME DEGREE

Blindingly Beautiful

Awesome is our uniqueness. Different we all are to some degree. Uniqueness radiates from the interior of our being. Sheltered and protected against the harshness of humanity. Tender in disposition. Some struggle with conformity whilst you peruse a more rebellious routine.

Smile I do at the efforts taken when you just need to be yourself. Your Light already shines uniquely you. You stand out in the crowd. You stand out with God. Child of God, you are favorite in His eyes just as you.

Rally I do in the uniqueness called you, for your Light is blindingly beautiful. Shine my friend. Vary your hair colors and paint across your face. Just remember, the grandest of all uniqueness is carried within.

Beyond the Darkness

Sadness fills my heart. Helpless I stand. From a distance I am kept. Wishing for a moment to simply hold your hand.

Change events I cannot. Your life has a course. Unique to you. Choices and lessons intermingled. Sometimes so difficult words cannot express.

Wish I could for one last time to hold you upon my lap. Rocking away life's ups and downs. Wiping away tears. Comforting your heart. Grieve I have. My job is done. Trusting in God that peace you will find in the world as you travel alone. Trusting that the pain you endure will quickly pass.

Pray I shall for angelic embraces. Guardians by your side. Lifting you up from your faltering stride. Holding your hand and heart when I cannot. Pray I will for you to suffer not from heartache, loneliness, hunger or want.

Trust, my child. A future of happiness awaits. Child of God. Child of mine. There is a grand journey ahead for you. For this I know to be true.

Beyond the darkness, God's Light shines.

CURTAINS TO LIFE DRAWN CLOSED

Puzzle of Many Pieces

What is it that draws you from your passion? So many talents. So many goals pushed to the edges. Not well fitted for the squared-edges of conformity. My friend, life is a puzzle of many pieces. Patterns of dark areas next to Light. You force situations to fit.

Stop the search. Connecting this to that. Frustration carried for the unknown. Missing pieces. Blaming. Searching. Curtains to life drawn closed.

Life, like a puzzle, is still whole. Some things will go unnoticed. Unanswered. Undone. But even spaces void are an integral part of the whole. There will be a time when all will come together. In the meantime, search no more. Let your life expand beyond the tightly formed border. Beyond the box of what you think or have been told. Let your life take on a different shape. Unique to you and your gifts. Throw to the side the squared-edging of conformity. Fill in your life puzzle one moment to the next.

Live life joyfully. Without the worry of where you are going. Let the puzzle fall from the edge. Expanding beyond your wildest dreams. When your Earth walk nears the end, you'll not care about a missing piece. The puzzle will be complete.

SPRING FLOWER

Perfection of God's Love

You are a beautiful spring flower amidst the thorns. Flourish you did through neglect. Unnurtured. Unadorned. Untended with the basics of love and tenderness. Struggled to thrive.

Yet you grow. Straight. Perfect in every direction. Perfection of God's love. Delicately embellished in rosy hues. God's Light cascading from a sunset sky. Reflection of innocence. Goodness to the core.

A perfect example of opted forgiveness and spiritual growth. Casting aside blame and unanswered questions of why. Some answers forever unknown. Unwavering you remain in faith. Unlimited greatness in God's glory. Reaching for the Light. Stretching the limits.

Beautiful spring flower. Gratitude I give for my path has crossed with yours.

RAINBOW-TINTED BUBBLE

Peaceful Journey

Preoccupied you are finalizing details before the journey unfolds. Many things left undone and untold. Hurriedly your mind races as the stomach rumbles. The twang of fear for the unknown.

I gift to you a bouquet of bubbles, rainbow colored and lavender scented. Tenderly tied with memories of life's joyful intersections. Feelings of unease quickly remanded with the release and pop of lavender recollections.

May your heavenly guardians remain close, protecting and guiding whilst nurturing your soul. Open yourself to Divine nudges.

When you feel the stomach rumble, pop another rainbow-tinted bubble.

Thorns of the Past

You're caught on a thorn. Wasting precious time. Haphazardly tugging this way and that. Tangled within a briar patch of the past. Unable to release from the thought-wrenching thorns. Holding you captive. Alone. Forlorn.

Small steps first, my friend. Gently release to God that of which you are caught. Untangle. De-thorn. You forge your destiny. Not the past.

Place one foot forward. The other will follow. Only look back to see how far you've traveled.

LOVE

Transcends Distance

I am here. You are there. Embraces relegated to phone and Internet parley. Matters not for the space of time or distance. Matters not the location in which you reside. When the moments of missing begin, hold close the satin-wrapped memories of life.

My love for you is freely given. Embrace life fully as I once embraced you. My love for you transcends the distance between nations.

As time and distance sink in, remember one thing. Love is the connecting force that binds. Love is the connecting force birthing life. Love is the answer to suffering and mayhem. Love is the reflection of God within. Love offers forgiveness to the guiltiest of souls. Love, when freely gifted, spreads laughter, peace, and joy.

Love transcends the distance between nations.

Boldly Praying

Standing in grace I clearly see. Souls searching for hope through graying skies. My friend, hope remains. Visible. Free. The dimmest Light can clearly be seen. A beacon shining. Parting the foggy trails. Hope for the basic of necessities. Hope for the unity of hearts. Hope for peace.

Compassionately speaking. Loudly singing. Boldly praying. Speaking. Singing. Praying. For peace. Unite as one heart. One breath. Around the world. Regardless of religion, creed or location. Boldly speak, sing and pray for peace.

Gift the greatest and freest of commodities. Hope.

COMPASSIONATELY DRIVEN

The Art of Faithful Living

The greatest gift you can give yourself is forgiveness compassionately driven. Forgiveness without duress. Forgiveness silently presented to yourself or another.

Forgive the harshness of decisions made. Consequences paid. Forgive ignorance from sleeping souls. Forgive hurts granted unintended or malice-driven.

Sit within yourself. Visualize forgiveness to yourself. Then offer it to another.

For within forgiveness you will find the art of faithful living.

WORDS AND ACTIONS

Peace Joy Compassion

What a troubled world we live in. When did it all go wrong? When did we lock our doors and hearts against our brethren?

Preachers, speakers, writers, teachers . . . share your heavenly messages. Worry not if you are degreed in theology. Are you not degreed in life? Are you not degreed in God's Light?

Look to the Light for guidance. Guidance will come.

We are all preachers, speakers, writers, and teachers.

Share goodness, peace, joy, and compassion through your words and actions.

WOUNDED SOULS

Purity of Grace

You were sent for a reason. A mission of utmost importance. Tattered and wounded souls to heal. The greatest gift to the planet is yourself. Purity and strength braided with experience. One lesson left to learn. Finish healing yourself.

Challenged, tormented, and tempted. Vicious cycle. Caught up. Then put out. Dragging alone along a crooked rocky trail. When will enough be enough? When will the vision of your Light outshine paths formerly taken? The vision sympathetically swaddled of yourself. You carry the past like a newborn child. Let it go. Embrace it no longer. For what you seek is that which you shall find. Deficiencies or purity of grace. When letting go of the skewed view of who you are, you will *come to be*.

Child of God. Perfection to your core. Look for it. Strive for it. Be it. Recognize it. See it in your actions. Feel it. Challenges, torments, and temptations will cease to be.

Heal yourself. Your gifts are truly needed.

Matched Set

I wish I could do more. Change of reality. Step back in time. Alone you sit. Wedged between breath and solitude of grief. Family and friends frequently call. But fill the void they cannot. For when a matched set is broken, life's pieces scatter across the tiled floor.

When you are ready, sweep together the remnants of what is left. Memories. Goals. Dreams. Wishes. Live the rest of your days making things happen. Show strength and fortitude, for you gift important life lessons to the next generation.

This Earth walk seems an eternity. For now hold in your heart-place the meaning and grace of life. Together you again shall be. Promise given from God. A promise reunited you will be.

Contagious to Generations

Strength is not determined by the weight you carry on social networks or corporate ladders. Strength is determined by the path taken.

Stand strong in your convictions. Stand strong in your faith. Stand strong in your ideals that one person can make a difference. Stand strong in the knowledge that this world can be a better place.

Put your efforts where they count. Live your life gifting and teaching. Live your life by example. Live your life lifting the spirits of others through words and actions. Live your life as God intended. Child of God, you are here for a reason.

Leave an imprint that transcends time. Larger than social media. Higher than corporate ladders.

My friend, leave an imprint contagious to generations. Child of God, you are here for a reason.

BUTTERFLY'S EXISTENCE

To the Helm You Hold

Winds prevail. Threatening the course. Distractions. Interactions. To the helm you hold. Consumed with purpose. Determination your guide. You've been rewarded. You carry God's Light.

Living in the moment. Gratitude given. Shining brightly. Nudging sleepers from their shadowed slumber. A butterfly's existence.

Flutter lightly throughout this day. This day gifted and unlike another. Hold your course. Gently nudge then wake another.

GIVE ME A HUG

Strength will Flow

Come, give me a hug. For I see your stockpiled sadness sits close to your heart. Matters not the source of your distraction. Clusters of interactions, misunderstandings, and heartfelt tugs.

Come, give me a hug. Combine our energies into one. Lean on my shoulder, let your tears run. Then rise above the cluster. Strength will flow. Face the dawn of a new day. You'll not be alone. I'll be here waiting, ready to give another hug.

CHILDHOOD FRIENDSHIPS

Love in the
Purest Form

Concern I have for world in which we live. Impatient arrogance against circumstances that are different. Different love, life, education, social status, and religion. When did we begin to own what was learned instead of what is natural?

Children love in the purest form. They know not of cars, houses, the color of skin, degrees, or religion. They seek friendship with their heart with the purest of intention.

If only to harbor child-like innocence again. Unlearn the impurities of learned distinguishes. Unlearn the recognition of color, race, notions, and perceived deficiencies of any order. If only to seek with your heart.

Love as a child again, reflecting purity and innocence. Together we can change our world one heart at a time. Hold my hand. I'll show you how it's done.

SORROW EXPANDS

God's Promise

Sorrow expands. Filling your heart. The suffering of a loved one clinging to life. Miracles nonexistent. Your compassion at odds with the heart. Hard to let go.

My friend, hold tightly to God's promise. Life continues.

Your loved one will live in the space of your heart. Through the breath of the wind. Through quiet times from within.

Release to God suffering and heartache.

Time to let go. Hold tightly to God.

GARDEN OF PEACE

Trumpet God's Light

The ego's wall of protection varies in thickness and layers. Justifications. Twisted intentions. Past indignations compounded with self-righteous behavior. Lashing back with words and actions. Hurtful lyrics tossed and cultivated.

Take down the layers of protection. Release the need to hurt back.

Surround yourself in God's Light. Take a breath. Let go of quips and jabs to the brow. Make a different choice or change direction. Turn not the other cheek. Just turn and go. Remove yourself from unsettling circumstances.

Take a breath. Replace the wall. Cultivate a garden of peace instead.

LIFE'S MELODY

Music to Your Ears

Exhaustion drips from your brow of indecision. Which way to go? What path to take? The heart pulling in one direction. A boisterous voice from the stands pulls in the other.

Money . . . money . . . money rings loud and clear. Stiff-backed bystander screams in your ear.

Tell me, dear one. What chimes the sweetest melody? Music only your ears can hear. Listen carefully.

Judge yourself not by the ego-laden standards of the other. Focus on the sweetness of life's melody. Strum your song to your heart's beating.

Child of God. You are here for a reason.

DISTRACTIONS TAKEN

Life Gifted

Recognize you I do not. As of late, distractions you take. Numbing the hatred for the journey taken. Cold, wrangling words of situations twisted. Difficulty sorting blessings from debris. Skewed self-gratification laced with flagrant disregard for life. Your life. Life gifted.

Child of God. Take not for granted the gift of a day. The blessings of God. If unhappy you are with the direction of your life, *then change!* This path you walk was forged with the choices you made.

Lift up from the wallows of self-pity. Take action. Take God. Give gratitude. Start small. Then give gratitude for obstacles and hard right turns.

Child of God, your talents are desperately needed. Wrangle words not to cause harm but for the greater good of all.

BIRTHING A STORY

Words for the Writer

You carry your manuscript like an unborn child—close to your heart, always on your mind, and with risk of going long past the due date. You fear releasing the precious cargo carried so gently and privately to critical eyes and sharp tongues.

But, as with a newborn, is it not your duty to yourself and God to gift the inspired words to the Universe? Suffer the laborious pains of revision. Grant your tender cargo breath and life. Release your words to seed within the heart and imagination of another.

Revise and let go.

Go through the process with determination, gentleness, and the knowledge that your beloved characters will soon have life.

Or, if you so choose, suffer labor beyond what is required as you relentlessly search for imperfections.

Birth your story . . . then be ready to conceive another.

Passing of a Friend

Uncomfortable is the grieving heart. A home once full now echoes emptiness. Too many years. A matched set. Now broken.

The passing of a life partner is a terrible loss. Grief takes over. Flooding the heart. Your time will come. United again. Until then, pick up the pieces and start anew.

Start small. A smile perhaps. A welcomed hello. A teacup alone has a purpose apart from the set. Give gratitude for what is left. An early morning walk. Fresh air. Each breath. Give gratitude.

When your walk has reached the end, a promise God gifts.

AMAZINGLY BEAUTIFUL

Child of God

You are riddled with rampaging thoughts of low self-worth. Birthed from the angry words of a bully of the lowest form. Stomping your dignity. Leaving behind a flickering Light on a battlefield-torn heart.

The damage inflicted is the burden of the other. Angry actions have a way of circling back.

But if your heart-field remains barren—you have but yourself to blame.

Turn from the words so hurtfully spoken. Bury them alongside the remains of the ailing relationship. Plant new.

You are amazingly beautiful. Child of God. Look in the mirror. See not what was said.

God does not make junk!

God made you.

SALVATION

Faithful Devotion

Let me embrace you. Welcome to salvation. Wipe away tears of emotion. For when God enters your life, you see the Light. Emotional complexities run rampant. Fullness of heart. Tears for the unjust. Realization of hurts delivered. Intentional or not. My friend, seeing and knowing are just the beginning. You are awake.

Welcome to peace and tranquility. Words and actions for the greater good of all. Joining in unison the love of God and brethren. Share your Light through faithful devotion. Laugh. Be joyful. Be grateful for blessings and paths traveled.

Blessing it is to be awake. Compassionate actions dictate. Remember, through your actions God radiates.

HUMANITY

Of the Father

Humanity. Spread across Earth Mother. Like the limbs and roots of a great oak tree. Traveling the planet. Borderless. Crossing seas.

Acorns drop from fingers of branches extended. This new sprout, related to the others. Of the same Father. As are we.

Embrace your uniqueness whilst remembering your brethren of different faiths and colors. All are of the same Father.

Embrace your brethren. Love their uniqueness. Love shared as a unit-of-one for the Father.

WEIGHT OF THE WORLD

Butterfly Graces

The weight of the world you carry upon your back. Of family. Of things undone. Of fears hauled from the past. Of hopes slipping away. Successes just short of fingertips callused and worn. What holds you back?

Look to your ankles shackled with doubt. Doubts of your worthiness. Doubts of your abilities and talents. Doubts more than I can count. My friend, the restraints are in your head. One step forward is all that is needed. One step forward on this journey of life. Have faith in your abilities and your connection to God.

More worthy you could not be. Child of God. Beautiful in your heart. Beautiful in your intentions. You are here for a reason.

Set free your butterfly graces. Set free the amazing person I know you to be. Set free the power within. Fly butterfly. Fly. Be all that you can be.

CONNECTION TO GOD

Peaceful Shores

A storm threatens peaceful shores. Gaining momentum. Masked in authority. Propelled by power afforded by money. The time is now to ready your abode for disasters personal, financial, and political in nature. Reinforce your faith and connection to God.

Remain calm and steady in your beliefs. Look to God's Light when tensions arise. Remain faithful. Stand true to your values. Stand true to your faith. Regardless the climate, live a peaceful existence.

Unite in prayer regardless location or religion. Unite as children of God seeking a peaceful and joyful existence—that is your God-gifted right.

Storms dissipate when passing over land. Do not feed into a negative climate. Surround yourself with friends and family strong in faith. Surround yourself with friends and family seeking a peaceful and loving existence. United as one we will withstand all storms—personal, financial, and political in nature.

DECADES OF SLEEP

Believe

Fearful you have been. Fearful of going without. Fearful of not measuring up. Release messages of unworthiness. Child of God. Your talents are needed. Goodness radiates from your core. Blinding beauty. Innocence in God's Light. Release dark and consuming memories. That was. This is. Peace will come. Stress will leave.

Grand abundance is but around the corner. Believe. Shake the earthly bindings of unworthiness from your feet. You are free. Free to live in the moment. Free to reap joys and pleasures. Free to be.

Rally in abundance. Employ latent talents surfacing from decades of sleep. Walk free. Surrounded in God's blessings.

TIME WASTED

Learn the Lessons

I understand. Been there myself. Many times. Countless moments rolled and twisted. Time wasted. Wringing of the hands. Wishing to change what was. Barrels of should-have-beens stacked and harbored.

Time turned back is not the place for your energy. Focus on the now. What is. What can be. A life full of opportunities awaits the open heart. Open mind. Open thought.

Protecting the now eliminates the barrels harbored. This moment is a gift God has granted. Unique. Like no other. Let go of rolled and twisted moments passed. Learn the lessons. Then let go.

PEACE THROUGH GOD

Healing Laughter

My heart aches for your burdensome journey. Questions unanswered. Slapped in the face. Defenseless and alone. Caught in the crossfire. No peace. Just strife.

My friend, God has not left your side. Gift of laughter you've been graced. Healing for yourself and others. Easing the passage of this life's challenges and heartaches. Free to use. Anytime. Any reason.

Laugh in spite of strife. Laugh at yourself. Laugh through life. Laugh until your belly aches.

Laugh through tears. Peace is on the other side.

PRAY FOR GUIDANCE

Lighten the Load

I have not the answer to uncertainness. Circumstances vary. Reasons sometimes untold. There are times when life is consumed with unsettledness.

Pray for guidance. Let God lighten the load. May you be gifted strength. Personal drive. May you progress through life's challenges with the greatest of ease. In harmony with nature, the Heavens, and earthly memories.

Personal dynamics and interactions come and go. No judgment. Compassion required. Lead by example. Strong in mind. Strong in body. For the greater benefit of your heavenly soul.

Pray for God's Light to see you through. The distance of headlights is all that is required.

WORTHY OF LOVE

God's Graces

Worthy you are of God's love and graces, regardless the distance traveled on crooked trails.

Worthy you are of God's love and graces, regardless the silenced voice echoed through thought.

Worthy you are of God's love and graces, regardless the hardened heart turned cold from the roughness of life.

Worthy you are of God's love and graces, regardless the twisted intentions and motives of others.

Worthy you are of God's love and graces, regardless your color, creed, or nation.

Worthy you are of God's love and graces, regardless of beliefs that differ.

There's room and space in God's heart regardless of who you are. Regardless the motives of sisters, brothers, mothers, fathers, children, or neighbors. You are worthy of God's love and graces.

Recognize your birthright. Hold onto your Light. Allow your worthiness to shine.

EMOTIONAL UNREST

Serenity

Peaceful you were. Serenity in solitude. Then circumstances unraveled. Unfolding of dynamics. Personalities clashed. Elastic memory of why you left. My friend, the past is the past.

Forgiveness dictates. Remembrance of times better spent. Look to the core. The heart-place where God resides. Impossible to hate or hold anger. We are all children of God. We are of the same breath.

Let go of the ego-driven impulses. No need to get even through words or actions. Leave to God the emotional unrest. Replace conflict with respect. Respect for another. Respect for yourself. Respect for this day gifted. Serenity need not be in solitude. Serenity is a way of life. Serenity is the peace felt with God in your heart.

ABSENCE OF LIGHT

Peaceful Blessings

Darkness takes over in the absence of Light. Anger envelopes the heart-place. Seeding mistrust. Teetering the line where harmony existed. Unrest. Swaggering through life ready to fight. My friend, so much easier an existence could be had if you would merely open your eyes.

Open your eyes to the blessings at your feet. Open your eyes to God's Light. When open to God's love, anger dissipates. Surely life provides challenges. Emotional unrest to new or uncomfortable situations. Bring Light to your heart with patience and gratitude for the blessings in hand.

The rough time will pass. Look to the Light.

GIFT FROM HEAVEN

See Clearly

You rush from the mirror's frustrating reflection. Pulling and tugging first this way and then that. Clearly seeing every fault magnified or imagined. You question. From whom was this high forehead gifted? And these ears and chin sharp enough to chip ice. Years pass, pulling and tugging. Trying to hide imperfections.

And then the beauty of life unfolded. A baby was born. Birthed from your body. A shining angel with a high forehead, pointed chin, and angled ears. Perfection. The most amazingly beautiful gift from heaven.

The next time you rush to the mirror for a frustrating reflection, before pulling and tugging, think differently of yourself. Birthed you were from God's breath. A shining angel with a high forehead, pointed chin, and angled ears. Perfection. See clearly, every beautiful aspect of your physical and spiritual being.

Child of God, do not disrespect the Father that gifted your life. In His eyes, you are the most amazingly beautiful gift from heaven.

SPIRIT OF A WARRIOR

Footprint across the Sky

I am sorry for your loss.

Life's bitter turn. Spirit of a warrior. Humble heart. Riding a golden-winged eagle to Heaven. Leaving behind a gap time will never fill.

Compassion to you and your family as well. May your loved one's energy for life continue.

Look to God's gifted sunrise for your loved one's footprint across the skies.

HURTFUL ACTIONS

Radiant in God's Light

Bruised is your soft-shelled exterior. Battered from the hurtful intentions of others. Eyes swollen with tears. Enough to fill a million oceans. Unevenly beats a delicate heart. Not enough Light to be seen.

My friend, sadness need not be your passage of life. Let not the actions of others dim your Light. You were born to shine.

Reflect the image of you, not the shadowed existence of others. Be within the divine space of your existence. Glorious. Amazing. Radiant in God's Light.

Step up from your knees. Stand tall. Stand in the knowledge that you are loved beyond all measure. Beyond the measure of time and place. Beyond the measure of this lifetime. Beyond your frail imagination.

Search for strength within your heart. For it is there that you will find God.

Let not a person, action, or intention dim that which you have been gifted. You are a child of God. Take your place on the throne of humble greatness. Reflect not the shadowed existence of others, but God's Light through pride in yourself and your actions. Pride in the compassion afforded to the planet. Pride in the compassion afforded to yourself.

My friend, you were gifted breath. Shine.

TOLERANCE WITH LOVE

Pulse and Breath

Tolerance is not enough without love.

Matters not the place from which we come. Stations set on platforms of gold or sodden earth below. Different we are in colors, nations, and religions. We travel the distance together.

See with your heart that which is blinded from sight. The pulse and breath of God in every soul. See with your heart. Recognize God's Light.

Tolerance with love is simply—*love*. We travel the distance together. Journey onward, my friend.

WALLOWING IN THE PAST

Forgiveness

God's blessings I send, for worry I have for the decades spent harboring judgment and wallowing in the vomit of the past. Ravaging happiness dropped by the doorstep. Wasting the precious life God gifted to you. My friend, no guarantees the distance or time on this earthly path. Open your eyes! Give gratitude. Gratitude for this moment in time.

When caught in the cycle of things done, look to the now. The beauty of another day ending or just begun. Gift to God the memories recycled.

Start small.

Forgiveness of hurts or transgressions. Then forgiveness to yourself. Forgiveness for wasted time looking back. Forgiveness for taking without giving to the whole. Gratitude will then follow.

One pass is all we have.

PUREST OF FORM

God's Love

Hurriedly you run. From this situation to the next. One step ahead of the needs of others. Placing yourself last. On the *always* list of offering assistance. Stop where you stand. Let me introduce you to yourself.

Circumstances have been that love was bought. Affordable for those that do and then do without. Bought through the intentions of how much and how well you can do for someone else. When love is bought, it is not unconditional. For unconditional is just as it stands. Love gifted without reason or action. Simply for existence.

Through the events of your life, love was ordered. Presented on a platter. Like a holiday bonus after a year of hard work. My friend, that was then. This is now. The circumstances have changed.

Let go of the egotistical persons that demand of you before offering their tokens of love. Let go of the feelings of unworthiness that plague your heart. For you have always been loved for just being you.

God loves you in the purest of forms. Truly unconditional. For you need not say, do, act, look, or be a certain way. God loves you for the essence of your being.

So, my dear friend, let me introduce you to yourself. You are a spiritual being graced with wisdom and love. A universe of love is reflected through your spirit and back. No penalties for books unwritten. No penalty for wrinkled skin. No penalty for not walking or talking fast enough. You are the perfection of Him. You are loved. Unconditional twinkling light harmonized with God's gentleness.

Sit with yourself. Get to know who you are. Silly you, you've been loved all the while.

FAITH

Courage to Follow

Life is like the sea. Sometimes calm. Other times rough. When calm, tendency is to float on a raft of daily routines. Never venturing off course. Faith dragged on a dingy of shored boards.

But then there are days when high-rolling waves pound relentlessly. Jarring those routines and challenging the faith haphazardly towed.

You have a choice. Stay put. Clinging to what you know. Or find courage. Climb on board with faith and travel directions anew. The choice is yours.

GOD'S STRENGTH

Alone You are Not

Suffer needlessly I wish not for you. Brace yourself against my stance. Strength I have. Broad shoulders to withstand. Wrap your arms about my neck. Together we'll walk. One step at a time. Scanning for Light.

And when the burden is too great for two, to God we will relinquish the yoke to pull.

Alone you are not. By your side I'll remain. If lost momentarily, remember God's strength supersedes eternity.

Acknowledgements

I am forever grateful for my connection with God.

Thank you Timothy C. Smith for sharing gifted time and life's adventures.

To my son, Timothy J. Cassano, thank you for the constant reminder to stretch my vision and abilities.

Thank you to my beloved Aunt Nancy for unconditional love and endless encouragement.

Thank you to final readers Kathy Scorse and Victoria Visiko for offering words of encouragement, insights, and reviews.

Thank you to my special writing groups for your heartfelt support. We have traveled over the mounds and furrows of mental barriers holding hands and hearts. You are the keepers of the secrets to life and the dreams of tomorrow.

I would like to thank my publicist, Denise Cassino, for her guidance on and off the page.

Thank you to Chris O'Byrne and the formatting team from *JETLAUNCH* Book Design for a wonderful experience and fantastic finished product.

A special thanks to Debbie O'Byrne from *JETLAUNCH* Book Design for another amazing cover.

I am forever grateful for the intersection of your paths with mine.

With warm regards,
—Sharon CassanoLochman

Index

www.ingramcontent.com/pod-product-compliance
Lightning Source LLC
LaVergne TN
LVHW051834080426
835512LV00018B/2865